Work From Home,
Teach English Online

by Edwin Buller

While every precaution has been taken in the preparation of this book, the publisher assumes no responsibility for errors or omissions, or for damages resulting from the use of the information contained herein.

WORK FROM HOME: TEACH ENGLISH ONLINE

First edition. July 4, 2019.

Copyright © 2019 Edwin Buller.

ISBN: 9781078258401

Written by Edwin Buller.

Contents

Introduction	**5**
My Story	**8**
PART 1: Is Teaching Online Right for Me?	**11**
1.1 The online teaching sector	11
1.2 Qualifications	15
1.3 Pay	19
1.4 Holidays	23
1.5 Equipment	26
1.6 Traveling while teaching	31
1.7 Summary of part one	33
PART 2: The Virtual Classroom	**35**
2.1 Who are the students?	35
2.2 Virtual classroom arrangement and mechanics	37
2.3 Classroom content	38
2.4 Lesson preparation	41
2.5 Feedback	42
PART 3: Teaching Principles and Methods	**44**
3.1 Online teaching principles	44
3.2 Online teaching methods	49
3.3 Parent expectations	56
3.4 Student expectations	57
3.5 Time management	59
3.6 Activities and games	63
3.7 Nerves	67
3.8 Mistakes to avoid	68

PART 4: The application and interview   **69**

    4.1 Your CV   69

    4.2 The application   71

    4.3 The interview   72

PART 5: Teaching as a career   **76**

    5.1 Getting paid   76

    5.2 Tax   78

    5.3 Online English teacher communities   80

    5.4 Looking after yourself.   81

Appendix: List of top ESL companies   **83**

Introduction

The English teaching market has skyrocketed over the past few years. Education, particularity in Asia, is booming, and the demand for proper English pronunciation training is high. The trend of using a laptop and the Internet to teach students remotely is set to continue to grow, and with it comes opportunities for teachers to take control of their schedule and employment, work from the comfort of their own homes, and earn up to $28 per hour.

But many teachers struggle to overcome the common pitfalls that prevent them from achieving the elusive fully booked schedule and finding success as an online teacher.

It is not a case of sitting down in front of your PC and expecting the bookings to roll in. There are a number of key strategies that you can implement to deliver engaging and effective lessons, designed to provide maximum value and enjoyment for your students, and allow you to become a highly rated teacher who is turned to again and again by the students, parents, and the company you work for.

This book will act as a guide on your journey to becoming a successful online English teacher. Success in all aspects, not just a high booking rate, a full schedule and professionalism in your interactions with your students, but also by providing key insights into the industry and how to work hand in hand with the way the systems are set up.

This book will outline how the sector shapes up as a job and a paid role. It will guide you through the idiosyncrasies that the Blogs and Youtube videos overlook. You will discover the key principles and methods of teaching online, classroom management, student engagement and retention. It will help you to choose the right company for you and take you through the application and interview process, how to get paid without losing exchange fees, and how to avoid the common mistakes that new teachers make.

By the end of this book you will have everything you need to teach English online and achieve the working freedom of a fully booked schedule that alludes many teachers within the industry. You will be able to relax - fully confident in your teaching abilities and the value that you bring as a successful teacher.

This book Is structured in parts and can be read in order, or you can dip into the chapter you are most interested in straight away.

PART 1. Is Teaching Online Right for Me?

This section provides insights into the online teaching sector as a whole and will help to clarify if the job is right for you. It is a precursor to the specific tactics that successful teachers use and discusses pay, holidays, equipment and qualifications.

PART 2. The Virtual Classroom

What does teaching English online look like? In this section we are going to look at the practical basics of teaching. Who the students are, what the virtual classroom and the content you will be teaching looks like, and what sort of feedback you will be expected to give.

PART 3. Teaching Principles and Methods

In part three we will explore the principles and methods of teaching English online. This is an in-depth guide to the mindset and techniques that successful teachers use to engage students, impress parents, gain a high teacher rating and a full teaching schedule.

PART 4. The Application and Interview.

Part four will guide you through the application and interview process. We will first look at the different companies available and talk about choosing the right company for you. We will talk about your CV and the application process. We will discuss what the interview looks like and end part four with the common mistakes that teachers make, and how to avoid them.

PART 5. Teaching As a Career

In part five we will discuss the maintenance of a successful teacher. How to get paid without losing exchange fees, how to pay tax as a freelance teacher, where to find supportive teacher communities online and generally looking after yourself for a sustainable career.

Happy teaching!

***

Please note, this book contains some affiliate links to services and teaching companies that I recommend and use myself.

My Story

I first started teaching English online in 2018 following a previous twelve months spent in Vietnam where I taught in private and state schools in real classrooms. Now that I was back home in the UK, I was looking for a job. I wanted to work from home, with time to spare for my other projects. I wanted enough money to support myself with some left over to save. I decided to continue my teaching career online.

I was nervous, because I was not sure how my real-world teaching experience would transfer into the online-world. The idea of teaching students in a virtual classroom was exciting, but I had so many questions. I had an understanding of teaching methodology, yet I still felt out of my comfort zone.

As it turns out, most of the skills needed as an online teacher were completely new to me. While my real-class experience was fantastic and certainly helped, it was very different than teaching 1-4 students at a time in an online virtual classroom.

Before I applied to my chosen companies, I learned as much as I could about the online teaching world. I read blogs and watched Youtube videos. I learned what these companies expected from their teachers and then I applied to two of them. I interviewed, and received two job offers. I started teaching with both companies, but I soon left one of the companies in favor of another, since I preferred the payment system and content they provided.

I soon developed the core principles and methods outlined in this book. My schedule began to fill and my students renewed their courses with me each month. I have now been consistently fully booked with the same students ever since. I know what to expect from each lesson and I don't need to think about work outside of my teaching hours. It is a perfect job for me, since it comes with a high hourly rate and allows me to spend my remaining time elsewhere - such as writing this book!

Surprisingly, teaching online feels more personal than my classroom based teaching. Even though the students are far away from me, I get the chance to spend more time teaching them as individuals. I know their personalities, and how to keep them focused. I know their strengths and where they need to develop. The more time I spend with them, the easier the lessons become. And the best part is that the more fun that I have in my lessons, the better, since this engages the students and keeps them coming back.

But it's not always easy. I have seen teachers who struggle to manage their classrooms. They don't understand how to balance effective teaching with engagement or how to satisfy parent's expectations. They can't retain their students and their schedules are only half booked because of it. Teaching can be exhausting, and It's a juggling act in a way. You need to engage and entertain the students while making sure they are learning and that the pace of the lesson is within the time constraints. It does have the potential to become stressful and overwhelming and at the end of it there are not the same opportunities to catch up with other colleagues and problem solve or let off steam at lunchtime as there are in a physical school.

These are some of the reasons that I decided to write this book. Because teaching should be fun and rewarding. It can and should be almost effortless since you are teaching something you have already mastered (the English language).

Within this book you will find detailed information aimed to guide you through the difficult areas where teachers often get stuck. I have compiled a list of questions commonly asked by beginner teachers and answered them from my own experiences and those of my colleagues within the sector. I hope you find it useful.

PART 1:

Is Teaching Online Right for Me?

1.1 The online teaching sector

Teaching English Online is the method of using a computer to teach the English language to students remotely over the Internet. You will be responsible for guiding the students through the lesson's content in the form of images, slides, and activities. You will encourage them to speak by sparking discussion and practicing sentence patterns, grammar rules and vocabulary while correcting their grammar and pronunciation.

There are a number of different options for how you can teach English online. You can teach adults or children, you can find your own students, or let a third party company provide the students and content for you.

The most common way of teaching English online, and the focus of this book, is through a company which is situated in the home country of the students. This company will host a virtual classroom, provide content tailored to the student's level, and connect you with the students, between one-four students per class. This is the best option for most new teachers since this way most of the heavy-duty admin and organization is fulfilled by the company and all you need to do is show up and teach.

11

If you wish to find your own students you can do so through paid advertisements on Google or Facebook. You will then create a content plan based on the students needs which you will teach using software like Skype or Zoom. With this method you have the most control over your freelance business. You can set your own price and dictate the progression of the content. However, this is not the easiest way to get started in Teaching English online and most teachers who go this route have years of experience under their belts.

What times will I teach?

If you elect to work for a Chinese company, like most teachers do, then your teaching hours will fall between 6pm and 9pm Beijing time (GMT+8). These are the times when teachers are in highest demand. This means that If you live in the UK then the hours are 10am-1pm or 11am-2pm depending on daylight saving time. If you live in the US then these times are much earlier in the morning.

Some companies allow you to teach students outside of these popular times, and you can find an extensive list of these companies at the end of this book, including companies with students from all over the globe. For example, the phone-based app, **Palfish**, allows you to take pay-per-minute calls from Chinese adults as well as teach regular content to children with more flexible hours.

There is a huge variety of companies available. If you are looking to teach English online full time, then you will want to choose a company with the most hours available and, ideally, a tiered payment system where pay increased for milestones of teaching hours reached. If you are looking to go part time then you will want to choose the company with the highest starting pay.

You can find more information about the various companies at the end of the book in **Appendix: List of Top ESL companies (page 81).**

Do I need to speak the primary language of my students?

In short - no. Most companies do not require their teachers to speak the primary language of their students.

It seems obvious that being able to speak your students primary language would be beneficial. You could easily translate concepts and new vocabulary and keep the students' attention with a sharp command. However, the purpose of these lessons is for the student to learn English. If the student has the option to speak their primary language then they will default to it. Your employer, the language company, and the student's parents, want the students to speak English only in the lessons. Therefore, you are not at a disadvantage by only speaking English.

Do I need to know every grammar rule?

No, you do not need to worry about knowing all of the English grammar rules. As a fluent English speaker you have enough of an understanding of grammar that you can correct the students when necessary. The students can learn the rules from their Chinese English Teachers and from books more efficiently than they can from you. Your job is to help them practice and cement these rules. You will also have an opportunity before each lesson to review the content you will teach so that you are never caught out.

Sometimes, students may surprise you by asking about a new grammar rule in the middle of a lesson. If this happens to you, and you do not know the rule off the top of your head, then a discrete Google search will quickly bring up the rule so that you can then explain it. This is most likely to happen with older student learners who are looking to get the most out of their lessons.

1.2 Qualifications

As of May 2019, Chinese authorities have made mandatory rules that all foreign teachers of English as a second language (ESL) to Chinese students will require a Teacher of English as a Foreign Language (TEFL) certificate. This certificate is quick and cheap to obtain online and you will find more information on TEFL certificates later in this chapter.

Some companies also require teachers to possess a bachelor degree or above. Some will accept teachers who are in their final year of study. If you do not have a degree then there are still a number of options for you. You can find more information on companies that do not require a four-year degree at the end of this book in **Appendix: List of Top ESL companies (page 81).**

It is worth noting that if you hold a degree or qualification in teaching then there may be more opportunities with higher pay available to you outside of the ones mentioned in this book.

When you apply to your chosen companies, they will often ask you about any relevant experiences you have had working with children, or teaching in general. Most companies do not require you to have direct teaching experience and it's very easy to glean some relevant talking points from whatever experience you may have. This is discussed further in **chapter 4.1: Your CV (page 67).**

It is also worth noting that some companies require you to be eligible to work in the US or Canada since that is the accent they wish their students to learn. If, like me, you are not from these two countries then there are plenty of other companies for you.

General Requirements

- TEFL Certificate
- Native English speaking teacher
- Have a PC or MAC with high speed and reliable Internet connection (Some companies allow you to use a tablet or smartphone)
- The ability to accept payment through bank wire transfer or services such as Paypal and Payoneer
- A positive attitude
- Some relevant experience as a teacher or working with children
- a photocopy of your passport and degree certificate

Do they hire non-native speakers?

The main value that you bring as a teacher is your pronunciation and therefore, companies are often looking for native speakers. Sometimes companies will hire non-native speakers if they currently have a low number of teachers employed. There are also some other options for non-native speakers who have a good command of the language, such as the website Italki.com. You can find an extended list of companies in **Appendix: List of Top ESL companies (page 81).**

Type of English Teaching Certificates

There are three types of teaching certificates that are most common. For new teachers I would recommend the TEFL certificate. It is the minimum required qualification by most companies mentioned in this book, is the cheapest and fastest to obtain.

TEFL (Teaching English as a Foreign Language).

This is the most common ESL teaching certificate. The process to attain one of these online qualifications usually involves completing several units of content followed by multiple choice quizzes and a lesson plan at the end. It can take anywhere from a weekend to a week to complete, plus the time it takes for the TEFL company to mark your lesson plan.

You can almost always find a cheap TEFL course deal on Groupon. You should pick one up for cheap ($20-40). There's no unified and universal standard for the quality of TEFL courses so don't worry about accreditation. While a TEFL can teach you some valuable teaching skills, it will not replace actual classroom experience.

TESOL (Teaching English to Speakers of Other Languages)

Another very common ESL teaching certificate. Similar to TEFL, there's no universal standard curriculum for it. TESOL tend to be offered by more accredited university-level organizations and as a result can be more expensive.

CELTA (Certificate in English Language Teaching to Adults)

This is an accredited certificate offered by Cambridge University. This is probably the most intensive English teaching curriculum you can obtain and universally recognized. However, it comes with a high price tag, plus in-person teaching experience and is widely considered overkill for online ESL teaching.

1.3 Pay

The hourly rate for teaching English online typically ranges from US$15 – 26 per hour, depending on the company and your qualifications. You can earn up to $28 per hour by teaching large group classes, but this requires a lot of energy and is uncommon (More information in the **Appendix (page 81)**). As a general rule, you can expect to make around $20 per hour. A typical 12 hour work week for me would net me between $1100 - $1450 in a month. I have seen and personally know of many teachers who work 20 - 30 hours a week and bring in $2000 - $3000.

Note that the standard payment currency is United States dollars $. This is very common within the ESL industry and helps international teachers to benchmark the pay rate between companies. You can use Google to find the current exchange rate and thus your hourly rate in your local currency. It is easy to get paid in USD even as a non-US based teacher. To find out how see **Chapter 5.1: Getting paid (page 74)**.

The pay structure is commonly like this:
Base pay per class + Bonus - Penalties = Actual Pay.

The base pay per class is a flat rate awarded upon the completion of the lesson. Some companies increase base pay when you reach certain milestones such as the completion of a hundred lessons. Your interview performance can affect the base pay offered, however this is not usually the case and most companies have a flat rate for all teachers. You can find the key qualities that recruiters look for in **Chapter 4.3: The Interview (page 70)**.

Bonuses are also common within the online ESL industry. They are usually rewarded around once per month, or at the completion of a unit. To be eligible for the bonuses you will need a good track record of showing up to class on time, and good feedback from the students and parents and a high booking rate, or student renewal of the unit. **Part 3 (page 43) is where you can find the Principles and Methods used by successful teachers.**

Most companies also have penalties. If you are late to class, absent, leave early or require leave without notice, then often you can be penalized, sometimes in the form of simply not receiving your bonus, or in a decrease of your pay.

All companies have their own compensation structure which you can use to your advantage. How much you make as an online ESL teacher will depend on which company or combination of companies you choose as well as if you reach the criteria for the bonus structures. Some teachers opt to work with two separate companies so that they can reduce the risk of losing hours by adding extra hours elsewhere. Other teachers will focus on just one company with an aim to maximize their bonuses by reaching milestones such as 500 lessons taught.

It is worth noting at this stage that some ESL companies do not like you to work with other companies. They may mention this at the interview stage and you may find It within your contract. Whatever you decide to do, It is important that you read about the different companies and choose the one which suits you. For an extended list of teaching companies see **Appendix: List of Top ESL companies (page 81)**.

Fluctuations in Pay

Pay for an online ESL teacher tends to fluctuate from month to month. You are an independent contractor, your own boss, and it is up to you to arrive on time and complete the lessons. If you take time off in a month, or you do not meet the requirements for your bonus pay, then you should expect your overall pay to be lower. There are also mandatory holidays such as Chinese New Year and Christmas, where you will not be working, and so will not receive pay.

Depending on the season, too, bonuses can rise and fall. In high season, from April to December, where there is more demand for teachers, the bonus pay offered by some companies is higher. It is then reduced slightly in the following months. However, these changes are small and the real key to a consistent paycheck is the have a fully booked schedule.

In **Part 3** (page 43) you will discover the principles and methods of teaching ESL online that guarantee happy students and parents and result in a full and consistent schedule.

How long until I get paid?

Another concern that new teachers need to be aware of is the length of the hiring process for online ESL companies. It can be quite lengthy. For me personally, it took six weeks from my application until I received my first paycheck. This is because most companies will pay between the 10th and 15th of every month, for the previous month. So if you started teaching on the 1st of the month, then you would not be paid until the 15th of the next month.

However, some companies pay more frequently than that (you can find more information in **Appendix: List of Top ESL companies (page 81)**. Overall, it is important to make sure that you have a source of additional finance to cover your bases for those six weeks.

1.4 Holidays

The question of holidays is a pertinent one for online teachers. There will be times where you need time off for vacation, visiting family and general emergencies which can arise at any time and require you to put down the headset and let someone else take over your class.

These companies are working on their own country's calendars and so If you are teaching Chinese children then you will be on the Chinese work calendar. Therefore, there is no recognition of British bank holiday dates, or most western holidays in general. You need to be aware of this and decide if working when your friends and family are enjoying a break is acceptable to you.

Often, you can expect mandatory time-off during the week of Chinese new year and most companies will provide a break at Christmas time for their western teachers. This varies by company though, since some companies continue with lessons at all times, regardless of the time of year.

The truth remains that time off is one of the most common grievances for online ESL teachers. It is important to remember that these companies are serving their customers, the students, first and foremost. This means that if you can't be there for your lesson then someone else will be.

Why is this important? We remember that since we are independent contractors, there are no employee benefits such as paid leave. Surely then, if you book time off, the only effect will be that you don't get paid. Not exactly. Booking time off can also have other lasting consequences.

23

What will happen when you book time off will depend on which company you work for and the specific circumstances. If you work for a company where you teach regular "units" to regular students then time off is a major detriment to the students learning. As a result, these companies are often strict with time off (just like regular schools). The companies and parents value commitment and regularity and variations to your schedule are deemed disruptive.

With these companies, if you need emergency leave with limited warning you can expect to face potential penalties such as 10% of your monthly salary or loss of your bonus pay. You may even lose those students. Even if you book your holidays in advance, you might still lose your students because the companies do not like to move the students between teachers frequently.

However, some companies offer a completely flexible schedule. You can open and close your slots at will, even an hour before your lessons, and you will not experience any penalties except that you will not be paid for that particular lesson. The down-side to these companies is that you won't be teaching regular students and this means you can't build solid relationships, which contribute to rewarding work. It also means that you don't have as much control over your booking rates, since a well taught and great lesson won't bring students back and you will rely on the company to book your classes.

Do you expect to require an ultra-flexible schedule with regular time off or do you think you can meet your schedule requirements? You should take this into account when choosing the company that is right for you.

Contract Lengths

Most companies offer contracts to their teachers of three to six months in length. At the end of this period you will be either asked to renew your contract, or not depending on your teaching performance. If you use the information in the following chapters then you will not need to worry about this. You will deliver amazing lessons, your students will love your classes, and contract renewal should be guaranteed.

If you wish to take a break between contracts then often the company can freeze your teaching account until your return. The repercussions will depend upon your company. Some are entirely flexible while others will be less so. You should expect to have less bookings to start when you come back, but again, if you follow the teachings in this book then you are bound to have a full schedule again in no time at all.

1.5 Equipment

There are certain items that are necessary as an online
ESL teacher. You will need a decent computer, a good
Internet connection and Ethernet cable, a headset, a
webcam, and a clean background. Some companies allow
you to teach using a mobile phone or a tablet instead of a
computer.

As well as these essentials, you could purchase some
props. Puppets are always a nice idea for teaching
children. The following lists are my recommendations for
solid and recognized equipment within the ESL industry.

Computer

You will need a computer. As previously mentioned, there
are some companies where you can make good money
teaching through an app on your mobile phone. **(See
Appendix: List of Top ESL companies (page 81))**.

If you choose to teach with a computer then your machine
will need to be able to run basic video calling programs
such as Skype.

The recommended specifications are:

- At least 4gb of ram although 8gb would be
  preferred.
- I5 Processor or higher
- Ethernet port preferred (although Ethernet to USB
  adapters are available)

These specifications are a guide. Check with your chosen
company for their minimum requirements as some
companies require much higher specs than others.

If you decide to purchase a new computer for teaching, remember to look for one with a built-in HD camera. Most laptops come with a webcam, but you need to check that the quality is high enough for online teaching. In order to deliver a high-quality video stream to your students you should check to make sure it is able to capture HD video in 1080 or 720p. Alternatively, you can purchase an external webcam.

Webcam

If you are looking to purchase an external webcam then the main specification is pixels and frames per second. Look for one that captures 1080p at 30fps or 720p at 30fps. Do note as well that many cameras list 1080p for screen recording, but when you look at the specifications for streaming it might run at 720p. Also make sure to check if the webcam will run on your operating system.

Best selling brand – Logitech ends up being one of the more popular brands. The model that has been one of the top rated with the best sales for some years now is the Logitech HD Pro Webcam C920, this is also the webcam that I use and recommend.

Headset

You will need a headset with a microphone. Most companies require this piece of equipment as it increases the quality of your audio, reduces echo and makes you look professional. USB headsets are often preferred by companies since their connection to the PC is more reliable.

27

A commonly used and highly recommended headset is the Microsoft LifeChat LX-3000.

Internet

You will need a good Internet connection. Typically minimal 5 MB per sec uploading and downloading. You are in excellent shape if you have over 20 MB per sec download speed. You can check your Internet speed online for free at https://www.speedtest.net/.

Many companies require the use of an Ethernet cable. If you are teaching on your mobile phone then you will not need an Ethernet connection.

The reason why some companies require an Ethernet cable connection is because it's very common for a WIFI signal to drop for a split second. This is something that you would never notice in normal browsing or Youtube, but can cause issues when streaming video. With an Ethernet cable your Internet speed isn't much different, but the stability of the connection is much better.

Will the company notice if you don't have an Ethernet cable? It depends on the company. Some of them run checks through the teaching program to ascertain how your computer is running and connected to the Internet and will email to ask you to use a cable.

Background

You will need a plain background when you teach. Many companies will ask that you keep your hair, clothing and background plain and professional. They do, however, appreciate some child-friendly decorations. The general aim is to reduce distraction, look professional and immerse the child in the English learning.

Some teachers teach with a wall behind them, others pull a curtain across and teach with that as a background. You can also use a green screen, since they are cheap and easy to set up, and some companies even require their teachers to use them. Combine a green screen with the software "Manycam", and you can turn your background into anything!

Here are some ideas of wall decor for a learning-friendly background.
 "Teacher (your name)" in colorful print and tacked to the wall behind you.
Shapes, letters, basic words. Like 'square' and 'fish' 'flower' and 'space shuttle'. Similar images and words to what you would find in a children's book.
The company's logo.

Good lighting is a must. Work near a window if it is during the day or use a lamp, or selfie ring light if it is at night.

Clothing

Your clothing should be comfortable, professional and child-friendly. You do not need to wear a dress shirt to every lesson. A T-shirt is fine. Many companies seem to favor a light blue T shirt as their recommended uniform but any plain T shirt will do. Don't wear your pajamas since that would be seen as unprofessional.

Props

Props can be a great way to reduce lesson monotony. When you sense that a student's concentration is waning, this is the moment to pull out a prop and bring them back into the lesson. Here is a list of popular props to use. You don't need to go overboard with them. One or two is often enough.

Anything of interest to you: Musical instruments that you play, pictures on your wall, local food items.

Hand Puppets: I use one or two hand puppets on occasion, through not every lesson. Some teachers go the DIY route and make their own while others find it easier to buy them online or in local stores. Having at least one puppet around will help keep most students interested in the lesson. I picked mine up at my local second hand shops.

I also use a cheap crocodile dentist game where you push in the crocodile's teeth and occasionally it bites you. The students love this, especially when you pretend that it genuinely hurt you.

White board - I use a small dry erase white board for drawing pictures, games and reward systems. This helps to engage the students and puts them in the mind-set of being in a real classroom. I don't use it every lesson but it certainly comes in handy and it was very cheap.

Flashcards – letters, pictures, etc. Great to test a student's English level and keep them on their toes.

1.6 Traveling while teaching

It is possible to teach online while traveling. You might be looking to teach as a way to fund your adventures, or as a way to maintain your schedule while away from home on a short trip, or visiting family and friends. However, there a number of concerns to take into account to do so successfully, including items you will likely want to ensure that you have with you.

- A quiet space
- A Laptop
- A strong Internet connection (Ethernet if required by your company)
- A portable background
- Props
- A lighting ring light

A popular way to travel while teaching is to use Airbnb or similar website where you are provided your own room or space. For the Internet, a very important component to online teaching, you will need to email the host of the property ahead of time and double check your Internet connection speed. The best way to do this is to ask the host to run an Internet speed test and to send you a screen shot of this with the date included, ensuring that it meets your companies' requirements. You will also need to take your laptop with you.

For your backdrop you can use a clean wall with sticky tack decorations such as your companies' logo. You will need to bring these decorations as you travel. To be extra safe against the possibility of your apartment not having a suitable wall as a backdrop, you could bring your own. Felt material is extremely lightweight and compatible and a large 4x3 foot piece is more than enough to serve as your backdrop.

You will also want to bring with you any props that you use including puppets or flashcards. Since there may not be any window close by a cheap selfie ring light can go a long way to ensure that you always have adequate lighting.

1.7 Summary of part one

So, is Online English teaching right for you? In this, the final chapter of section one, I will summarize the main points that have been discussed.

There are a multitude of reasons why becoming an Online English Teacher is so appealing. It allows you to manage your own schedule, work anywhere in the world with a reliable Internet connection, build relationships with your students, and earn upto $28 USD per hour. You can enjoy teaching without the constraints of an institute or other classroom settings and aside from giving feedback, all of your time will be spent on actual teaching. You wont need to find students or plan your lessons.

You will usually be hired as an independent contractor by the company, so you won't receive full-time employee benefits. You will need to take care of your own health insurance bill, if you are in the US for example.

The time difference can be off putting for many teachers. If you are based in the US and teaching students in China, then you will be teaching early mornings since the prime teaching hours are 6pm-9pm Beijing time (GMT +8).

While the pay is good, you will likely make just a part-time income from teaching. However, there is always the option of going full-time if you think you can handle it. Some teachers work 30-40 hours a week and make upwards of $3000 a month. Make sure to choose your companies carefully as some have more teaching hours available than others.

If you want to have regular students then you will need to stick to a schedule, just like in real schools. If you are absent then a substitute teacher will take your place. Depending on the company and the situation, this can often result in financial penalties or losing your class. Some companies are more flexible with holidays and cancellations than others.

Teaching has always been a rewarding profession and teaching online opens the door for everyone. You have the opportunity to positively impact and genuinely contribute to your students' lives. At the time of writing I have over twenty students whom I have taught twice a week for the last nine months. I have built trust with these students. I have seen, and been a part of, their developing language skills. Through my relaxed and fun lessons they have gained an awareness, and hopefully appreciation, of western culture which they may not have gained elsewhere.

Indeed, the more fun you have as a teacher, the more your students will enjoy your lessons. If you have fun while teaching then the students will want to come back and learn with you. Combine this with some solid teaching practice, which you will learn in the following chapters, and the parents will be happy too. Your schedule will be full and your income will be sustainable. Now, let's learn the basics of the virtual classroom.

PART 2:

The Virtual Classroom

2.1 Who are the students?

Most of the companies mentioned in this book focus on teaching Chinese children. This is because the majority of the online ESL student base comes from China, and most of those are children, typically between the age of four to sixteen years old. If you wish to teach students of different ages and locations then please refer to the **Appendix: List of Top ESL companies (page 81)**. You will also find that most of the teaching methods and principles outlined in section three will still be relevant and helpful for these students.

You can expect to teach, per class, between one and four students at a time. Your students will typically be very well behaved since obedience is a top priority of the educational system in China, and their parents are paying money for the lessons.

Often, the parents will be present with the children during the class, especially if the child is very young or if their English ability is very low. If the parent is not with the child during the lessons then they will usually have access to the recording of the lesson afterward. Sometimes the parents will remain completely quiet during the lesson, but other parents will be vocal, chastising the student for not speaking or knowing the answer. This is something to be aware of as an online ESL teacher since the parent is a paying customer there is little you can do about this. While it can be frustrating, it can also help keep the child focused and participating in the lesson.

2.2 Virtual classroom arrangement and mechanics

So, what will the virtual classroom look like?

Normally, each online ESL company provides their own software through which you will teach and therefore utilizes a slightly different virtual classroom layout, which will have different mechanics and functions that you can use within your lessons.

There will be small square video streams of you and your students, which you can move around. Your cursor will act as a pen, which you and your students can draw with, and you will have the option to mute your students and prevent them from drawing or interacting with the screen.

Some companies use face filters, like the Snapchat dog, which you can use to entertain and engage the student, making the classroom more child friendly and holding their focus. One company that certainly uses this feature is **Palfish**, the phone app. Other companies may allow you to use the Manycam software which is incredibly versatile and entertaining, if a little expensive.

Most companies have some form of reward system to promote good behavior. Images will flash up on the screen "Great Job!, Creative Idea!"

Some companies have virtual dice which you or the students can roll. Most companies also provide a countdown timer which can be immensely helpful in encouraging competition and overall increasing student engagement and speed. In **Section 3: Teaching Principles and Methods (page 43)** we will discover how to use the various classroom accessories, such as the dice and the timer, to our advantage.

2.3 Classroom content

The teaching content varies depending on which company you work for. The company will set the level of the content based on the English level of the students. They will also choose the curriculum and the topics. Some companies are reported to have better content than others. The company **SayABC**, for example, has content created alongside The National Geographic. This content is a joy to teach and the primary reason why **SayABC** is the company with whom I personally teach.

Typically, you will be provided with between 20-35 slides and a time frame to get through them. Most companies have a fixed schedule, but some allow you to work at your own pace and carry on from where you left off. It is standard practice to allow teachers to access the classroom content at least a few days prior to the lesson so that they can prepare.

Some students, typically older or more advanced, prefer to ignore the content altogether and simply have a conversation with you. You should check with your specific company before doing this, to see if it is allowed.

Forms of content

I will now outline the most common forms of English content. You will find that each lesson you teach will contain some variation on the below forms of content. In the following section you will find detailed descriptions of the teaching methods to use for each of these forms of content **(Chapter 3.2: Online teaching methods (page**

48)) They are easy to master and you will only need to teach them once to develop your techniques.

Please also note: most companies provide extensive training videos to newly hired teachers, which are taken from real lessons. In these videos you can view typical content and the corresponding teaching methods. Youtube also has a number of useful videos. Search for "how to teach ESL online" to get started.

Phonics: These are the basic sounds we make when speaking the English language. "Mm, Nn, Oo, Pp" are just a few examples. Think of how you would pronounce "Oat" for the big O sound, and "Octopus" for the smaller o sound. What shapes and movements does your mouth make? Before every lesson you will have an opportunity to review which phonics sounds you will be teaching.

Sentence patterns: These are short sentences used to practice speaking.You will drill these sentences with the students until they can ask and answer each other without your supervision. It may take some guidance and encouragement from yourself until the students reach this point. Examples:
"Can you jump? Yes, I can. Can she jump? Yes, she can."
"Do you want a truck? Yes, I do. Does she want a kite? No, she doesn't."

Grammar: There will be grammar rules to practice with the students. As previously mentioned, you don't need to know every grammar rule. Your job is to help them practice and cement these rules.

Vocabulary with images: You will find that most lessons will have a vocabulary segment where new words are introduced and previous words are reviewed. Usually, these slides will involve moving segments and activities where you can play games with the students.

Quick Tip: If you are teaching more advanced learners, then you may be asked about the differences between British English and American English. The main two differences are spelling and vocabulary. There are hundreds of everyday words that are different. It is up to the students themselves to decide which vocabulary to use.

2.4 Lesson preparation

Will you need to plan and prepare before each lesson?

One of the great things about teaching ESL online, through a company that provides the content, is that most of the general management is handled for you. The company will plan, designate, prepare, host, collect the money and pay. All you have to do is turn up on time.

So, for most companies, you will not need to spend much, or any time at all, preparing lessons. Content is presented in a standardized format, which means that you will face similar slides in every lesson. After just a small number of lessons most teachers feel confident in their ability to deliver the planned content without preparation.

The most important piece of lesson preparation you can do is check that you understand the grammar rules and which phonic sound is being taught in that lesson. Grammar can be the trickiest part of a lesson to teach given all of the exceptions presently afforded in the English language. Unless you are a grammar expert you will not know all of the grammar rules off the top of your head. It can be very useful to have a Google page open when you teach, in case you need check your understanding of a specific rule.

2.5 Feedback

Many online ESL companies require some form of written feedback on the student's language abilities after you teach one or more lessons. How often this feedback is required will depend on the company that you work for, but writing feedback should not take up much of your time. Some companies require feedback after every lesson, others after every three, and some do not require it at all.

If your company does require written feedback then there will be a character minimum and maximum, between 200 and 1500 characters. In general, a paragraph of feedback is considered appropriate.

Feedback should reassure parents that their child is taking value from the lessons. It should mention behavior and attentiveness. It should summarize the content of the lesson including sentence structure, vocabulary, phonic sounds, and grammar rules. It should include any particular mistakes that the child makes consistently through the lesson. This could be mouth formation for certain phonic sounds or pronunciation of words. Perhaps the child is using singular nouns when they should be plural. Take mental or real notes of these during or directly after the lesson if you don't think you will remember.

A standard paragraph of feedback may look like this:

Sissi had a great lesson today, she remained focused and participated throughout. Sissi should continue to practice talking about the different ways we celebrate holidays, using the vocabulary from today's lesson "a parade, fireworks, a feast, a party, a costume, a mask, a lantern." and using past tense of regular verbs (+ ed) such as "danced, dressed up". Sissi did a great job pronouncing "usually" and should continue practicing this sound like I showed her in the lesson. Great work Sissi, see you next class!

PART 3:

Teaching Principles and Methods

3.1 Online teaching principles

Most teachers aim to make the most of the time they are able to devote to their work. They want to minimize gaps in the working day where they do not have lessons booked in but are available to teach. They aim to gain a fully booked schedule.

The principles of teaching outlined in this chapter are here as guides to keep you focused on the most important aspects of teaching English online. There are three main principles centered around creating valuable, fun and simple lessons. In the following chapter we will discuss the different methods that we can use as teachers to enact our principles, with an overall aim of keeping our students coming back for more.

If you follow the details in the section then you should have no problem gaining a full teaching schedule, which will allow you to take up teaching ESL online as a part or even full-time role. You will understand exactly what the parents and students expect from your lessons. Your routine will become fluent and enjoyable, and you will be able to jump into each lesson confidently.

Principle 1: Pronunciation is key

The first principle on this list is about pronunciation. It is the component that successful teachers within this industry focus on in order to create the most value for their students.

You should always focus on eliciting speech from the students, correcting their pronunciation, and repeating the process.

The majority of the student base are using online lessons as a supplement to their main English language learning. They are spending time in school during the day learning English with a local teacher who speaks English as a second language. This English teacher has likely mastered English grammar and, unless you are a grammar expert, it may be the case that this teacher has a better working knowledge of the idiosyncrasies of the English language because of their training and daily practice whereas our grammar knowledge is intrinsic, and often difficult to describe.

On top of this, their local teacher has translation abilities and textbooks. So, it's difficult for us to teach our students grammar more effectively. But what that teacher is unlikely to be able to do is pronounce words like a native speaker. This is one of the greatest values that we bring as an online teacher of ESL.

If our students want to pronounce words properly, they might be confined to the Internet, movies, and other media. But those mediums do not provide instant verbal pronunciation feedback like we can.

So, always remember that pronunciation is key to creating maximum value for your students. When the parents see their children overcome the pronunciation hurdles that their primary language places on them, they will love you for it.

Principle 2: Keep it simple

This second principle is all about keeping your lessons simple, for yourself and the students. Imagine that you are trying to learn Chinese, and that you have just begun to understand some basic vocabulary. But then a whole sentence is thrown towards you, with grammar and syntax and plenty of words you have never heard before. It is easy to become overwhelmed when learning a language and when you become overwhelmed a barrier to learning has been created.

Each lesson that you teach will be part of a broader learning unit. It will contain content designed to support the content in the following units. You should aim to stick to this content closely, to the vocabulary, grammar rule and sentence pattern of that day. **This will stop your students becoming confused, and will increase their feelings of satisfaction and achievement, which will keep them coming back.** Trust the content. Rome wasn't built in a day and neither is the ability to speak a language. The units have been created together as building blocks.

As a very minimum, make sure the student understands the content and can pronounce the words or sounds, and then move on. At the end of the lesson, and if you have time, you can extend the content with activities, games or questions but if you only teach the content, then that is fine too. Just make sure that you do cover all of the content in the lesson. You can find time management techniques in **chapter 3.5 (page 58)**.

Another great way for beginner teachers to keep lessons simple is to think about the topics that your students are likely to know. Common themes in children's books, for example, are animals, food and toys. Think also about your word choices when communicating with them. Your students will be likely to know and understand the word "beach" but unlikely to understand "shore". If you stick to familiar topics and words when talking to your students then they are more likely to understand and enjoy your lesson.

Principle 3: Make it fun

The last principle on this list is about balancing your teaching focus to create fun and engaging lessons for the students. A huge mistake that many teachers make is to get caught up in the idea that lessons need to be perfect. They focus on maximum efficiency, cramming as much into as short a time frame as possible. It's certainly great to be efficient, and an overall good teacher, but If you don't allow your students to have fun then they will not want to be there.

Lessons are almost never perfect. Only occasionally do I shut down my teaching software and think - "that was a perfect lesson." But when this does happen it is because the students have been engaged and the best way to engage a student is to let them have fun. **It is hard to convince a child to listen and learn. The best way to do this is to make your lessons fun and so if you can manage this then you can be sure of your job security.**

If you fail to entertain your students then they will stop paying attention to you. They will take longer to answer your questions and this will throw off the entire pace and timing of the lesson. Suddenly the class isn't as relaxed because you are rushing through every slide with an eye constantly focused on the time. You will find yourself becoming tense, commanding the students to repeat sentences and not giving as much praise as your students are used to.

This is a portrayal of what can happen when your lessons are too heavy on English content and therefore not fun for the students. Remember that you are here for the long-run. There's only so much that you can teach in thirty or forty minutes. If the students come out of the class with some new vocabulary, sentence pattern or understanding of pronunciation, then you can call that a win. Just by being there and listening to you they will have gained a wider understanding of the language and how it sounds. To keep them listening the lesson should be enjoyable and lighthearted.

In the following section you are going to learn about the different methods we can use to entertain our students and keep them engaged.

3.2 Online teaching methods

In this chapter I will detail the various teaching methods that successful online ESL teachers use. These methods are established to help you to enact the three principles in the previous chapter. By using these methods you can be sure that you create engaging and effective classes that will keep your students coming back.

Total physical response

Total Physical response (TPR) is a teaching method informed by the way children first learn their native language and it is extremely beneficial for effective online teaching. When a child is still learning to speak their first language, parents have conversations with them. They give instructions and the child responds physically.

"Look at me," "give me the ball," ect...

These conversations continue for many months before the child begins forming words. Even though they can't speak during this time, the child takes in the language, including the sounds and the sentence patterns. Eventually, when the child's brain has decoded enough information, the child will begin to speak. TPR attempts to mirror this effect in the classroom.

At any point when you are speaking, giving instructions, introducing new vocabulary or any other time, you can mirror your speech with body language. If you say "jump", you make the action with your body or fingers. If you say "happy" then give a big grin and point to your mouth.

TPR can be adapted for all kinds of teaching situations.

- For vocabulary connected with actions (smile, chop, headache, wriggle).
- For tenses past/present/future and continuous aspects (Every morning I clean my teeth, I make my bed, I eat breakfast)
- Classroom language (Open your books)
- Imperatives/Instructions (Stand up, close your eyes)
- Storytelling

Successful ESL teachers always use TPR in their lessons.

Online English companies love it when teachers use TPR because it is extremely valuable for teaching and keeping your students entertained and engaged. It lifts the pace and the mood of the lesson and helps students to remember phrases or words. It is good for kinaesthetic learners who need to be active in the class and works well with mixed-ability classes. The physical actions get across the meaning effectively so that all the students are able to understand and use the target language. It involves both left- and right-brained learning and finally, TPR is especially useful for Online teachers since we face extra barriers of communication when teaching remotely through a computer.

Phonics

Phonics are the different sounds we make when speaking a language, such as Oo, Tt, Uu, Pp. The sounds of a language are often the hardest part to learn. Each letter, or group of letters, is made with certain mouth movements of the tongue, lips and teeth. We don't always realize as native speakers, but these mouth movements are very important. Most languages contain some phonic sounds that English does not, and visa versa. Phonic sounds are the key to fixing your student's pronunciation.

When your student mispronounces a word - underline the letter or syllable in the word on the slide - and pronounce the word again after the student has finished speaking. Make sure to give special attention to the particular sound where the student has made a mistake.

Lean closer to the camera and point to your mouth to show that is where they should watch and concentrate. Show them exactly what they need to do with their lips, teeth and tongue. Don't wait too long after they have mispronounced the word. It's better if the memory is fresh on their lips so that they can realize the mistake and how to rectify it. Now cup your ear with your hand to show that you are listening and it is the students turn to speak.

The "v" sound, for example, requires your front teeth to come over your bottom lip slightly.

The "th" sound requires your tongue to poke out under your front teeth.

The "w" sound requires your lips to make an O shape.

Practice making these above sounds. Notice how these sounds form on your mouth. Become excellent at teaching these formations and you will be adding huge value in your lessons.

Concept checking questions

Concept checking questions (CCQ) are questions designed to check your students understanding. It is important to use these throughout the course of a lesson.

Use simple questions to elicit a response and personify each question with hand gestures:

"What is it?"
"Is It a ___?" (You can get it wrong here so that the students correct you.)
"No, it isn't. It's a ..." (cup your ear so they finish the sentence)

You can also ask the students to demonstrate their understanding. In a physical classroom you might ask them to point to someone with long hair, but in the virtual classroom you might ask them to circle the picture of the girl with long hair.

You can use closed questions, with yes or no answers, to quickly check student's understanding. You can use open questions, with open ended answers, to spark conversation, test the English language ability level, and allow your student to practice what they already know.

It is a good idea to use concept checking questions in the "review" part of the lesson, or after you have taught some new vocabulary or grammar rules for the first time. However, you should try to ask these questions to your students as frequently as possible.

Get them speaking

In order to fix our student's pronunciation we need to get them speaking. You should try to get your students speaking English as much as possible. There are countless ways to do this, but one of the easiest ways is to use humor, if your students are children. One lesson I placed a book on my head and I asked my students, "Is it a hat?".

They will say "no". But we want them to speak full sentences so point to your mouth and said "No, it is a book.", now cup your ear and wait for them to repeat the full sentence. Afterward you can model the phonic sounds if they made any mistakes.

"A book?" Take it off your head and look at it "oh, yes. It is a book. What color is it?"
"Red"

"It is red." (cup your ear)

"It is red. (student repeats the full sentence)
"Do you like reading books?"

"What is your favorite book"

I have only included these questions to give you an idea how to keep a conversation rolling with students whose English is very limited. It is important to use very simple language, to incorporate TPR and humor to engage them, and overall aim to get them speaking as much as possible while correcting their language mistakes.

Don't take yourself too seriously in the classroom. We have all had teachers to take themselves very seriously, and your students will not be an exception to this. It's OK to be a bit clownish. If the children are speaking English and enjoying themselves at the same time then they will love the lessons and so will their parents. I attribute my ability to have fun in the class as to why the students continue renewing their lessons with me.

Blank students

You will encounter students while teaching who do not respond to your questions. This can be frustrating, especially since you are time-pressured and you are not in the physical vicinity of the student. There can be any number of reasons why a student will act this way, but the solution is often to change your activity.

This is a great time to bring out a puppet or a soft toy such as an animal. You can use these toys and puppets to model what you want the student to say by asking the puppet and answering the question, as the puppet. It may sound and look silly, but showing a student what to do is often much easier than telling them, especially if they know very little English.

You can also use TPR (cupping your ear to prompt them to speak, touching your mouth when you speak, leaning into the camera, etc.).

You can try clapping your hands. First, say the name of the student, then "look at me" or "pay attention" and clap your hands on each syllable. This will help to vary the pace and bring the student back into focus.

You can involve another student with strong English

abilities. Ask them to "help," and have that student be the teacher. They should try to elicit a response from the blank student, much like you would do. You can instruct the students like this, "Winnie, ask Fiona this." And then circle the question, which will be on the screen, that Winnie should ask so that Fiona finishes the sentence pattern. This often varies the feeling and pace of the lesson and gets the student speaking.

If the student does answer you, make sure to praise them and reward them with your company's reward system.

Frequently, you may still get no response and in these circumstances the best thing to do is move on to the next student. Realize that you can't win them all. Later on, give that student extra praise when they do answer you.

The Dice

If the virtual classroom of your chosen company includes a dice. which you can roll, then you can use this tool to randomly select which students will speak first and stop any students feeling left out. To do this, say the student's names and then the number assigned to them. If there are three students in the class they each get two numbers so a total of six. If there are four students in the class then I will assign myself two numbers (5 and 6). When a five or six is rolled and I get picked, I always pretend to be shocked and angry about it, which served to entertain the students, but really this just gives me an opportunity to model the pronunciation again.

3.3 Parent expectations

It is important to be aware of the expectations of the student's parents before we teach their children English. After all, they are paying for your services and they will often be watching the class live, or the recording of it.

What parents desire is for their children to learn English efficiently, and to have fun while doing it. Ideally you can teach their child a lot in a small space of time and provide some real value for money, but this is dependent on many factors including class size and time spent with each individual. It also depends on the content and if it is an appropriate level to the learner. There are many factors that can impact a student's learning in any given lesson.

At the end of every lesson the parents should think their child has a better grasp of the English language in some way. You should try to ensure that each child comes away from every class with some improvements to their English abilities. The best way to do this is to have your students speaking full sentences, when possible.

If you can provide a fun learning environment for your students, then the parents will be even more happy. Students work very hard in China and your lessons are an opportunity to provide a relaxed, engaging and informative time with lots of speaking practice.

One more, and often overlooked fact, of online ESL teaching is that your students are gaining cultural experience. The students get to spend one on one time with a western person and gain a wider understanding of life from a young age. So don't worry if your lesson isn't perfect because, from the parents eyes, the student is still learning.

3.4 Student expectations

As well as thinking about what the parents expect, it's important to figure out what our students want from our lessons. At the end of the day, if the student wants to keep learning English with you, the parents will be most likely to oblige.

Children usually come to your lesson after a rigorous day within the formal education system and often, they are tired. Your lessons should be relaxed and informal although you should remain professional at all times.

Most of the students are going to be between the ages of 4 and 16. They want to have fun in your lessons, but also they want to come away from every lesson feeling confident in their English abilities. It is therefore important to be patient with your child learners and keep the lessons simple.

It's about striking the balance in the lesson. On one hand you want children to behave like they would in school so that you can teach them as effectively as possible, but on the other hand you want students to enjoy your class so that they keep coming back. You should find a healthy balance between these two. If you are in doubt, err towards fun. If the child is speaking English as well as having fun then you will be doing a great job.

If you are teaching older students then often they will have their own agenda. They may ask you questions that are not to do with the content and you will need to think on your feet to answer them.

Knowing who our students, and their parents, are is a key driver of our success as online English teachers. We should provide both value in our teaching as well as a fun and relaxed environment. By focusing on these points, it makes easier to meet expectations, retain our students and maximize our time with a full teaching schedule.

3.5 Time management

Time management is an essential skill for any teacher and teaching online is no exception. It is often late-evening time in your students' home countries when you are teaching them. Therefore, parents may expect you to finish on time so they can put their children to bed.

In most scenarios, you will find yourself pushed for time. You will need to cover content quickly in order to have all students speaking and finish all of the lesson's slides on time.

There are several reasons why you might find yourself running out of time, but it all comes down to your progressions through the lesson content. Usually, there will be a number of minutes at the top of each slide which depict how long you should spend on that slide in order to stay on-time. Generally you will have between one and two minutes per slide. I pay almost no attention to this number and instead I look at the number of slides remaining and minutes remaining. If I am at 15/30 slides and I am through 30/40 minutes, then I know I need to hurry up. It is easier to manage my time this way since I can increase or decrease my progression through the content depending on how many minutes are left and how difficult the content is for the students. If the content is difficult you will want to spend more time on it than on slides with easier content.

You don't want to be rushed as a teacher because this can make you impatient with the students and then you will not teach fun lessons. In an ideal world, you will never be faced with the above ratio of slides to minutes, but it does happen. Especially If you greet your students at the beginning with questions such as "How are you?", and

"What did you do today?". If you do elect to do this, then you will need to make up for several lost minutes over the course of the lesson.

The only situations you can expect to have extra time are when your class sizes are small, your students are attentive, and they have good English abilities relative to the content. Unfortunately, this doesn't happen very often. If you do have free time, then at the end of your lessons you can stick around and chat to your students, or play games with them, since the virtual classroom does not shut down. But you should try to finish the content first.

How can we manage our time better?

The more you teach, the more familiar you will become with your company's content. You will learn where you can take shortcuts and which content needs more time spent on it. Time management will become more intuitive, but you will always need to be aware of it.

You don't want to skip entire segments of content. The curriculum is designed for the students to follow along to and they could miss vital learning opportunities if you do. Some companies may even punish you for doing this and so time management is an essential quality of a successful teacher.

However, do not be afraid to skim quickly over content you think they already know. When I first started teaching online I would ask each student five different questions about each slide. What color is it, what is this, what is that? Is it a ...? This is fine when you first begin teaching your students, but if you know that they know the answers already then don't waste time by repeating the same questions each lesson. You should move faster over those slides and focus on the new grammar rule introduced later on. It's almost always better to have students speaking full sentences. Simply make sure that they understand each slide by completing the activities, or check their understanding with concept checking questions, and move on.

You can have your students complete activities solo, in pairs, or all at once. Solo is preferable because you can give direct pronunciation feedback, but sometimes it is simply necessary to have all the students repeat the sentence together. Since we are teaching online their voices will be a jumbled cacophony so do your best to listen for mispronunciations, underline the word, and have all students repeat it again. Remember that the students can hear each other.

If the company you teach with provides some sort of timer then use it to speed your students up. "I wonder if Eric can say this faster than Nina?" (start ten second timer.)

There will be times when you feel annoyed at a student. Perhaps they are turning their camera off and playing games in the thirty seconds between questions and each time you ask them a question it takes five seconds of everyone waiting before they turn the camera back on and give a half-answer, meaning that you need to repeat yourself. This can become especially frustrating since time passes very quickly as a teacher. You will find yourself pushed for time to finish all of the content and so situations like the one above can be a big concern. The best way to deal with this particular issue is to write about it in your feedback so that the parents become aware of it. Try not to raise your voice in the height of aggravation. You can find some more time-management techniques in chapter **3.5 Time Management (page 58)**.

You can always mention behavioral issues with your feedback and hope that the parents ask the students to stop. However, this is up to the parents and the company. If they are happy with the child only paying half-attention, then you may just need to deal with it. This means that sometimes you will need wait for a student to come back into the lesson, and then repeat yourself. One methods of dealing with this situation effectively is, once you do have the students attention, quickly run through several slides of content with them and then do the same with your other students. Although not ideal, this will reduce the amount of time wasted.

3.6 Activities and games

On some occasions, you will find yourself with some spare time. Perhaps the lesson content is very simple, just a single word on each page, and is not suited to the student's English abilities and you fly over this content very quickly. ESL teachers in a real classroom would have a number of games and activities up their sleeves for this very moment, but it can be tricky in online lessons to engage the students and even to make them understand what this new activity is.

Believe it or not, having extra time is a great problem to have. I wish I had spare time more often. Usually, I need every minute to squeeze in the lesson's content and if I want to chat to the students I do it within the first few minutes of the lesson or after the time has run out, if the students stick around.

If you find yourself with free time often, then most likely the students are finding the content too easy. It is worth trying to come up with some more challenging activities for these students.

Below, you will find some examples of fun games and activities for online lessons. But before you decide to use them, you should decide if you are spending long enough on the lesson content.

Are the students pronouncing the words perfectly?
Do they understand the content based on the concept checking questions that you ask them?

Activities for free time

Overall, the best use of this time is conversation and pronunciation practice but If you really are struggling to fill the time then it is handy to have a toolkit of activities and games to fill the time and boost your student's English ability. Below are several examples of my favorite activities that work in online classrooms.

Teach a song, Happy and I know it, Wheels on the bus, Baby Shark.
Teach Days of the week, Months of the year.
Teach different foods or animals with TPR.
Bring out your white board and draw things, animals, vehicles, food. Ask them questions as your draw "What are they? They are wheels." "What is it? It's a Tiger."
Ask questions about themselves "What did you eat for dinner today?"
"What is your favorite animal/toy/food?" Students will be happy to show your their favorite toys and then you can ask them questions about it.

Games

If you still have spare time in your lesson then you can introduce games to fill those extra 5-10 minutes. Most of the time you will not have very much time to play any games but it is always fun to bring out the white board and marker.

You should try to tie in these games with the vocabulary from that lesson, and always encourage students to form full sentences. Either way it all comes back to getting the child to speak as much as possible.

Note that the camera may be flipped for the students, so that they read the words backwards. There isn't an obvious remedy for this except that you write the words backwards, which is difficult to do. I have never had any complaints and so I wouldn't recommend writing backwards. Make sure your handwriting is clear and review the words as you write them down so that they know the words that are on the white board

Hangman - A classic game that has the benefit of almost-global recognition. Many of your students will understand this game format without the need of explanation. I like to draw a staircase leading up to a cliff with shark infested waters below, instead of a noose. Each step represents a letter that the students can get wrong. A little man at the bottom will climb the stairs and eventually fall down to the sharks.

You can point at the man and as, "Who is this?" and then point at the students "It's you". Then you can ask "Who is this?" pointing at the shark, "It's teacher" then use TPR for biting motions with your hands saying "Teacher shark".

You should model the activity before playing, using a simple word like "dog" and guessing the letters yourself. Show incorrect guesses and correct ones, show the man falling to the sharks. This will accelerate student understanding.

Pictionary - Draw a picture with the students. Ask them questions about what you should draw next. You can draw anything, but often the favorite is to draw teacher. "Does teacher have a big nose?". The picture can become quite ridiculous and the children love it.

Tic Tac Toe / Naughts and crosses - Another classic, draw two grids on your white board and have the students recount the vocabulary from the lesson. Fill in one of the grids with the words and make two teams out of your students. Model the game by saying the words and filling the corresponding squares on the empty grid with an X or O when they are correct. This is a great way to review pronunciation.

3.7 Nerves

What if I get nervous during teaching or my interview?

It is normal to be nervous for your interview and mock class. Even with a year's experience in the classroom, I still had nerves. However, I stuck to the routine I had practiced and I landed both jobs.

The key here is practice. Make some bullet points for each slide that you will teach and then practice each slide using hand gestures throughout. Practice it several times. Even during these practice sessions you will have nerves but it is better to have them now. By the time it comes to teaching you will be a lot more relaxed because you have completed it five times before and now you are just showing someone. During your practice you can also record yourself. This is a proven technique to reduce nerves since it can simulate the same feelings that you may have during the real class and give you an understanding of where you can improve.

3.8 Mistakes to avoid

Don't show your mobile phone on camera. Place it on silent during your lessons and keep it out of sight.

Keep your environment clean and quiet. You should be the only person heard or seen on your end during the lesson.

Try not to get frustrated. If you are running out of time just move on to the next slide. It's better to keep a positive attitude.

Dress appropriately, a T shirt, shirt, or requested uniform is fine.

Give equal attention to your students and don't favor one student over another. Most of the time, when a student becomes upset, it is because they feel left out. This can also be one of the most difficult aspects of teaching. When the students' English levels are very different, you may feel that particular students need more attention and time to learn a topic, set of vocabulary, sentence pattern or grammar rule. But remember that these children's parents have spent the same amount of money on the lesson and each child should get the same talking time. Use the dice to select students fairly.

Have a glass of water nearby when teaching.

Own your mistakes! If you make an error then do not be afraid to correct yourself. Do not stick to your guns and teach your students incorrect language. Some experienced teachers even make errors on purpose to see if the students will correct them.

PART 4:

The application and interview

4.1 Your CV

Please note: There is a comprehensive list of companies available as of June 2019 in **Appendix: List of Top ESL companies (page 81)**.

Before you apply for your chosen companies, it is time to build your CV. Within your CV you will want to talk about your formal education, including TEFL certificate and any relevant experience you have working with children or teaching in any way. Be sure to note the minimum criteria for each company before you apply and make sure that you meet it.

Capitalize on any/all experience you have working with children and/or teaching. Some teachers include parenting, nannying, Sunday school, church, tutoring classmates in high school. It is unlikely that will ask you a lot of questions about this experience, but the important thing is that you include some experience working with children and anything that is remotely connected to teaching. At a push you could talk about customer service roles and how they demonstrate your patience and ability to communicate with others.

If you are lacking experience, then you could consider volunteering at a local school, or with a charity hosting special needs group sessions. However, this is not necessary and I would recommend applying first and including the experience you do have. The most important thing with these companies is how you do on the interview and mock lesson. If you have met their criteria, including TEFL certificate and as much experience related to teaching and working with children as possible, then you will more than likely be accepted.

Many companies ask for their teachers to hold a degree, although this is not always the case. If you do not have a degree then you can still apply for the positions, as well as the companies outlined in **Appendix: List of Top ESL companies (page 81)** who do not require a degree.

If you have been a tattoo artist, or if you have any tattoos then please be aware of how this may be viewed by the employer and the parents due to cultural differences. Teachers are typically expected to keep all tattoos covered because some Chinese parents do not think that teachers and tattoos go together. During your application and interview, do not talk about tattooing experience. Instead, you can say that you worked as a freelance artist, sketching customized artwork to fulfill customer request.

It is now time to apply for your chosen companies.

4.2 The application

The application process is similar for most of the companies in this book. You will be asked to upload your CV, or fill in fields on a form including where you are from, your expected teaching hours, and your teaching experience. Either way, you will want to have a CV with the right information prepared since you can copy information from that document into the form.

It can be a good idea to apply for a number of companies at the same time. As I noted previously, the hiring process can sometimes be lengthy and you don't want to have to start from the beginning three weeks later because one company didn't work out.

Keep in mind that at some point they will ask you to send a photocopy of your passport and degree certificate, if you have one.

4.3 The interview

After your application is accepted you will normally be sent an email with a list of available time-slots and you will be asked to book a time suitable to you. It is important that you show up on-time as being timely is a core attribute of an online ESL teacher. In the email you will also receive information on the format of your interview.

The interview is sometimes when your base hourly rate is discussed. Not every company opens this up for debate and most have a base hourly rate that is fixed. Be prepared to ask for the top end of their base rate as this demonstrates confidence in your own value.

You may be given the option of a live-demo class with a real interviewer, or for a live recording. Sometimes, the interviewer will ask you questions about yourself and your relevant experiences that are included on your CV, other times there will be no interviewer and no questions asked. The main priority of the interview is to observe your teaching skills, and following the questions will be a mock lesson or demo class.

The questions

You can expect most questions to be fairly simple. If you have read this far you then should feel confident that you meet the criteria for online ESL teaching and should answer these questions honestly. The questions will be about yourself:

Where you are from?
What qualifications do you hold?
What experiences do you have working with children?

You should have written some answers to these questions in your CV before your application. Make sure that you are confident talking about these answers before your interview. If not, go back and practice speaking your answers out loud until you do not need to read them from text.

The important thing to remember here is that the focus is on how you come across on camera. Your attitude and pronunciation are often more important than the actual answers themselves, within reason.

There are some key qualities that recruiters emphasize. Passion and energy, friendly attitude, smiles and patience, engaging actions including questions, tone of voice and body language with a professional outlook. Show up on time and don't wear your pajamas!

The Mock Class

Once the questions are over, it will be time for your mock class.

The mock class is where you demonstrate your teaching abilities. The company will notify you ahead of time on the content that you will teach and provide access to it so that you can practice. Sometimes, they will let you choose between two or three topics, but the content is always very simple, for example colors or animals.

The mock class will take between 5-15 minutes. In this time you will need to navigate the slides and teach the content on them. The mock class varies by company and sometimes it will be a live interview with an adult who pretends to be a child for the duration of the lesson, or it will be a recorded interview where you pretend you are speaking to a child.

I would recommend reading through the slides and familiarizing yourself with the classroom mechanics before the interview. Make brief notes on each slide about what it is you will say. What questions will you ask? For example, you might write

Slide 1: Model speaking the sentence then ask: "Can you say this?" while using TPR. Cup your ear (to show it is the students turn to speak.) Repeat the word, and underline the phonic sound, if the student makes a pronunciation mistake. Cup your ear. Next slide.

Go through the slides, practicing what you will do in the demo class. Repeat this process until you no longer need your notes and the process comes naturally to you. This is the best way to prepare for the mock classes.

A brief summary of what you should remember:
Do you speak clearly and with simple language?
Remember to smile,
The more lively and animated you can be, the better.
Use hand movements and TPR.
Use concept checking questions like "what is it?", "is it an __?"

The demo interview may seem intimidating but all you need to remember are the principles and methods outlined earlier in this book. If you have read this book then you are more prepared than the majority of teachers these recruiters see every day. They don't expect you to be perfect or polished and some nerves are to be expected.

The shy interviewer

A final note on the mock class. The interviewer, who is pretending to be a child student, will often act shy. They will be reticent, witholding their answers and sometimes pointedly ignoring you. They will try to give you a hard time so that your teaching experience does not flow like you expect.

The interviewers do this because they want to see how you would handle the situation. Are most students going to stare blankly at the camera and say nothing? No, but some of them are. Sometimes the students will even be upset.

Solution: What we do in these situations is remain patient, repeat yourself and use TPR. Try to change your method up slightly, use a prop, engage them in a different way if you need to.

PART 5:

Teaching as a career

5.1 Getting paid

Congratulations! you have earned your first income teaching English online. Your company will have already told you their chosen payment methods, so it's time to set them up. Payment for a typical month will normally come in the middle of the next month and will come through bank wire transfer or some service, such as Paypal.

Income can be lost from the conversion of currencies, or fees from transfer and services and this is something you should be aware of when you venture into the world of online teaching. Some companies require you to use services such as Paypal or Payoneer. These financial services take a fees out of your salary such as a 4% transaction fee on PayPal, or fixed $2 per transaction on Payoneer. Unfortunately, this may be the only option some companies provide.

Some companies, however, will offer to pay you in your local currency, thus avoiding fees or transaction and conversation.

Bank wire transfer

In some situations, fees can be avoided.

Traditional banks often charge a fee to accept a bank wire transfer from overseas. On top of this they often use an exchange rate which is not current and ends up costing you more. One way to avoid these extra charges is to use a service called TransferWise. It is a US-based online bank with very low fees. You can open an account with them from anywhere in the world, so even though I am based in the UK, this bank allows me to have a US-based account with them. TransferWise saves me a lot of money each month and I would certainly recommend looking into it. They convert money between currencies at the current rate, and they send funds to your main bank with very low commission.

Help out the author! Use this link to sign up for TransferWise and receive very low fees:
https://transferwise.com/u/edwinb68

5.2 Tax

Important note - I am not a legal or tax expert. The information included in this chapter is correct to the best of my knowledge but it is not guaranteed to be correct or up-to-date. Please seek professional advice and ask about legal and tax implications where you live.

Online English teachers are typically independent contractors hired by the company, instead of a full-time employee. Therefore, you will be responsibl for your own income taxes. Most companies do not deduct and withhold taxes from the teachers' monthly payment, but some do. These companies are the exception rather than the rule.

USA

For US citizens and tax-payers, all income of more than USD $600 per year is reported directly to the IRS via the 1099s form. The self-employment tax is 15.3%. Therefore, you must either save 15.3% of each paycheck or just figure out the grand total of your earned income and then multiply that by .153. That's how much you owe the government. It's worth noting that self-employment tax doesn't include the income tax. That's an additional percentage on top of the 15.

You can deduct business expenses as a self-employed contractor. The Internet, square footage of your home office, any supplies you bought such as a display board, stickers, wireless mouse and computer.

UK

For UK citizens, you should register for self assessment in order to work out the taxable pay and National Insurance contributions you are liable for. This is the case even when you have a second job, other than teaching online. Tax and national insurance contributions are deducted as you earn. You will find information on **gov.uk**.

5.3 Online English teacher communities

Teaching online can be a lonely job. Especially since you work from home and don't have any colleagues to interact with on a day-to-day basis. Fortunately, there are a number of places online where teachers congregate and support each other.

Usually, the company that hires you will have their own communities. Their Facebook pages are often filled with relevant content from other teachers and these are a great way to keep informed about changes in your company. It will also give you opportunities to ask questions of other teachers and find mentors. In my experience, these teachers are always happy to help.

Also, look at forums such as Reddit. There are a number of Subreddits there which can provide some excellent up-to-date advice about which companies are currently hiring and what might fit your specific needs.

5.4 Looking after yourself.

If you decide to commit to teaching for the long term, then there is more we can do to maintain our health and make sure our teaching is sustainable.

Sit properly: Sitting for hours at a computer chair without good posture can be very bad for your back.

Go outside: Since you are working from home, without frequent interaction with colleagues, some exercise or time outside of the house can be hugely beneficial to your mental and physical health.

If you find yourself not feeling up to the task of teaching on any given day, then the following simple exercise will allow you to relax and teach more effectively. The meditation alone clears your mind and helps you focus on what's important, which is better serving the student. It will allow you to have more fun and not worry about the small issues. I would highly recommend giving this simple exercise a go.

Before every lesson, I try to spend a minute, or even thirty seconds, with my eyes closed, focusing on my breathing. I sometimes try to see the world through my students eyes. It's night time, where they are. They probably had a long day in school. They see a small picture of you on their screen. They want to enjoy your lesson in a fun and relaxed atmosphere.

Did you enjoy this book?

I want to thank you for purchasing and reading this book. I really hope you got a lot out of it!

Can I ask you a quick favor though?

If you enjoyed this book, I would really appreciate if you could leave me a review on Amazon.

I love getting feedback from my readers, and my reviews on Amazon really do make a difference. I read all of my reviews and would love to hear your thoughts.

Thanks so much!

Edwin Buller

<u>Appendix:</u>
<u>List of top ESL companies</u>

In this section you can find the top companies in the online ESL space, as of June 2019. Keep in mind that these are not all of the companies available, only some of the prominent ones. However, this is an evolving industry and the information included here may be outdated at the time of reading. This company guide is intended as a foothold to assist in your own research.

To choose the right company for you, you need to decide if you want to work part time or full time. You will need to decide if you would like to teach adults or children, or both. You will need to decide what times you are available to teach. One way to increase your booking rates is to look for companies with a large number of students compared to teachers. The way to do this is to see which companies are advertising on job forum boards, through your TEFL company, and anywhere you would look for jobs. The companies who are advertising the most have a high demand for teachers and thus are more likely to fill your schedule.

You can use websites such as Online ESL Reviews and Online English Teaching Jobs as well as the multitude of Facebook groups out there to read other teacher's reviews and learn about their experiences with different companies to assist you in finding the right opportunity for yourself.

For companies that work with **adults,** check out the online ESL schools

- Englishdom
- Likeshuo
- Italki
- 51 Talk
- Palfish
- Cambly
- ITutorGroup

For companies that works with students **worldwide,** so that you can work almost any time, check out:

- Cambly
- LatinHire
- English First Online

In the remainder of this chapter you will find extensive details of some of the main companies working with **children in China,** which has been primarily discussed in this book. You will find their pay rates, potential hours available, qualifications needed and general Pros and Cons of each company. Remember to do your own research as the details may be outdated at the time of reading.

SayABC

Help out the author! Use this referral link to apply to SayABC: **https:// Tinyurl.com/yxcpnhcx**

Minimum Hours: Three.
Hours offered (Beijing time):
2 days/week (Monday/Thursday, Tuesday/Friday, Wednesday/Saturday)
6pm, 6:50pm, 7:40pm, 8:30pm.

Requires TEFL Cert?: Yes

Requires Native English Speakers?: Yes

Acceptable accents: North American, UK, Australian

Requires College Degree?: Yes

Requires you to live in a specific country?: No

Experience with kids/teaching required: Yes

Internet Speed required: 20 mbps down/ 15 up

Computer Specs required: Mac or Windows, at least an i5 processor, 8gb ram (officially it's 4gb but you will probably have IT issues and lose your classes with only 4)

Children or adults: kids

Company books lessons or Parents/Students book lessons: company

Regular students?: yes

Average time to be fully booked: Immediately - 2+ months.

Flexibility/cancellation policies: must give at least 4 hours' notice. If you miss 2 or more classes in a unit then you lose the homeroom bonus for that unit. Excessive cancellations will affect future bookings. Not very flexible company.

Group classes or individual: group, up to 4 students

Curriculum type and quality: National Geographic Our World. Excellent curriculum. 4 levels, 9 units each, 9 classes in a unit.

Class Length: 40 minutes, 10 minute break

Feedback Required?: yes

Browser-based, other platform-based, or company app: custom desktop application available for PC or Mac.

Pay Rate: $15/class + Homeroom bonus: $54 ($6/class) for hotslots $36 ($4/class) regular slots paid at the end of a unit (9 classes)

Sub: if you take over a homeroom part way through a unit you get $22/class and no end of unit bonus

Trial bonus: if a student signs up within 5 days of a trial class you get $8/student. Most teachers don't get many :(

Pay Methods offered and Fees: Wire transfer or direct

deposit.

Pay Frequency: monthly, usually between the 12 and 15 of the month

Referral Bonuses: yes

Offered Contract Lengths: 3 months

Itutorgroup

Help out the author! Apply to Itutorgroup at:
Join.itutorgroup.com and use code **BEBX**

Minimum Hours: Five

Hours offered: Twenty Four Seven

Requires TEFL Cert?: Yes

Requires Native English Speakers?: Yes

Acceptable accents: North American, UK, Australian, New Zealand

Requires College Degree?: Yes, BA in any subject

Requires you to live in a specific country?: No

Experience with kids/teaching required: Yes, 1 year experience.

Internet Speed required: At least 20 Mbps download

Computer Specs required: Windows 7, Windows 8, Windows 10 or MAC OS 10.8x

At least 4 GB Ram

Children or adults: Children & Adults

Company books lessons or Parents/Students book lessons: Company books lessons

Regular students?: No

Average time to be fully booked: Immediately - 2 months

Flexibility/cancellation policies: Very Flexible

Group classes or individual: Group and Individual classes

Browser-based, other platform-based, or company app: Browser

Pay Rate: To start - $14 - $22 an hour to start, rising to $18-28.
Pay Frequency: Monthly.
Offered Contract Lengths: 1 year but flexible.

VIPKID

Minimum Hours: None
Hours offered: 9 am - 10 pm Beijing Time
Requires TEFL Cert?: Yes
Requires Native English Speakers?: Yes
Acceptable accents: Neutral American
Requires College Degree?: Yes, BA in any subject
Requires you to live in a specific country?: You must be eligible to work in the US or Canada - but you can live in many different places in the world.
Experience with kids/teaching required: Yes, 1 year experience.
Internet Speed required: At least 20 Mbps download
Computer Specs required: Windows 7, Windows 8, Windows 10 or MAC OS 10.8x
At least 4 GB Ram
Wired Internet
Children or adults: Ages 4-14
Company books lessons or Parents/Students book lessons: Parents books lessons
Regular students?: Yes
Average time to be fully booked: Immediately - 4 months
Flexibility/cancellation policies: Can cancel 6 times in a 6 month contract
Group classes or individual: 1 on 1
Browser-based, other platform-based, or company app: Browser or app available.
Pay Rate: To start - $14 - $22 an hour. Base pay per class

(30 minute classes) $7-9 + bonuses of up to $2 per class.
Pay Frequency: Monthly.
Trial class conversion Bonuses: $5
Offered Contract Lengths: 6 months
Pay for standby time?: No.

Hujiang

Company: Hujiang
Minimum Hours: 10 hours/week
Hours offered (Beijing time): 9am to 10:30pm
Requires TEFL Cert?: Yes.
Requires Native English Speakers?: Yes
Acceptable accents:
Kids program: US, UK, Canada, Australia, New Zealand
Adults program: same as above, plus South Africa and Ireland
Requires College Degree?: Yes
Requires you to live in a specific country?: No
Experience with kids/teaching required: Yes for kids program
Internet Speed required: 10 mbps down/ 10 up
Computer Specs required:
Windows only
at least an i5 processor
at least 4gb ram
Children or adults: kids or adults
Company books lessons or Parents/Students book lessons.
Regular students?: if they book you
Average time to be fully booked? 1 month.
Flexibility/cancellation policies: You can choose your own schedule but must choose 2-3 weeks in advance. Must cancel at least 6 days in the future or get fined.

Group classes or individual: individual.
Class Length: 25 mins
Feedback Required?: yes
Browser-based, other platform-based, or company app: custom desktop application available for PC.
Animation level required: moderate
Pay Rate:
Kids: audio and video, $16 - $20/hr
Adults: audio only, $12 - $16/hr
Pay Methods offered and Fees: Payoneer. $3 fee for every deposit. Other fees for withdrawals. Must exchange to your local currency with their exchange rate.
Pay Frequency: Bimonthly, from 1st - 15 and 16 - end.
Offered Contract Lengths: 1 year
Pay for standby time?: no. classes can be booked in open slots up to 4 hours in advance

PalFish

Minimum Hours: No minimum
Hours offered: (Beijing time) 6 pm-9 pm Monday- Friday, 9 am -10 pm Saturday and Sunday
Requires TEFL Cert?: Yes
Requires Native English Speakers?: Native speakers required
Acceptable accents: Neutral accent
Requires College Degree?: No.
Requires you to live in a specific country?: No.
Experience with kids/teaching required: Some experience required.
Children or adults: Both children and adults
Company books lessons or Parents/Students book lessons: Parents book lessons
Regular students?: Depends on student choice.

Time to be fully booked: Depends on your lesson quality, we have teachers who get fully booked everyday.
Flexibility/cancellation policies: Teachers can cancel the appointments 24 hours in advance without a fine.
Group classes or individual: One on one class for 25 mins
Curriculum type and quality: PalFish provides materials and assistance to all the teachers
Class Length: 25 mins
Feedback Required?: Yes
Browser-based, other platform-based, or company app: Multi-platform(tablet, mobile phone and PC)
Animation level required: moderate
Notes on preferred teaching style: Show yourself, energetic, kid-friendly
Pay Rate (Please include how the bonus structure is broken down and what the average new teacher can expect):Make up to $22/hour+ Bonus($30 bonus when student buy a package after taking your Trial class, $15 bonus for buying props when you get started, $160 monthly bonus for TOP 10 teachers, $80 bonus for TOP 11-20)
Pay Methods offered and Fees: paypal, Bank transfer, payoneer ,wechat, alipay
Pay Frequency: once a month
Referral Bonuses: 200 RMB
Trial class conversion Bonuses: $30
Interview Process: Download PalFish Teacher app and apply from the app directly.

Qkids

Minimum Hours: 6 hours a week.
Hours offered: (times in Eastern Standard Time, EST) All days of the week: 6:40-7:10, 7:20-7:50, 8:00-8:30, 8:40-9:10 (All AM)

Friday and Saturday have additional night hours: 8:40-9:10, 9:20-9:50 , 10:00-10:30 , 10:40-11:10 , 11:20-11:50 (All PM)

Requires TEFL Cert?: No

Requires Native English Speakers?: Yes

Acceptable accents: US + Canadian

Requires College Degree?: You need to have a Bachelor's Degree or be in the process of obtaining one (enrollment in college/university)

Requires you to live in a specific country?: US or Canada

Experience with kids/teaching required: Some experience.

Internet Speed required: Minimum upload speed: 2Mbps. Minimum download speed: 4Mbps. Wired connection.

Computer Specs required:

Children or adults: Children ages 5-12 grouped by skill level

Company books lessons or Parents/Students book lessons: Company books lessons for you

Regular students?: You don't often see the same students again.

Time to be fully booked (in your experience): Not a whole lot of time! The first two weeks you are hired they only book half of your classes, and after that you have a full schedule. I've heard this depends on parental reviews but I'm not 100% sure how much that factors into it.

Flexibility/cancellation policies: Very flexible.

Class length: 30 minutes.

Feedback required?: No.

Group classes or individual: Classes range from 1-4 students.

Curriculum type and quality: High quality.

Browser-based, other platform-based, or company app: Company app.

Pay Rate: $16 - $20 USD an hour (2 lessons), each in-lesson time is 30 minutes. The base pay is $8 USD per lesson. You can also earn attendance bonus and performance bonus, $1 USD each, calculated weekly. With full bonuses, the pay is $10 per lesson.

Pay Methods offered and Fees: Direct deposit or Paypal.

Pay Frequency: Once a month around the middle of the month

Referral Bonuses: $100 for every successful hiree

Magic Ears

Minimum Hours Required: None required

Hours offered: 6:30pm-8:30pm and 9am-11am Monday-Sunday (Beijing time)

Requires TEFL Cert?: Yes

Native English Speakers?: Must be a native English speaker from USA/Canada

Requires College Degree?: Yes. In any subject.

Requires you to live in a specific country?: No.

Experience with kids/teaching required: Some experience required.

Internet Speed required: 10MB per second.

Computer Specs required:Windows 7 or later, Mac OSX 10.11 or later.

Children or adults: Children (4-12 years old)

Class length: 25 minutes

Feedback required?: Yes.

Company books lessons or Parents/Students book lessons: The company books the classes

Regular students?: no

Time to be fully booked: In the beginning you can only teach a limited number of hours. After you have taught your first 10 classes you can open all slots.

Flexibility/cancellation policies: No penalty for sick days or emergencies.

Group classes or individual: Up to 4 students per class

Curriculum type and quality: Interactive with songs and games.
Pay Rate: Base pay is $9-$11 per 25min class. You get a $1 bonus per class if you enter your first class of the day within 8-10 minutes early. You'll receive a second bonus of $1 per class if you open 60+ slots for availability per month.
Pay Methods offered and Fees: Paypal or bank transfer
Frequency: 10th of every month
Offered Contract Lengths: 6 month
Pay for standby time?: Yes. $5 + bonuses for being on standby

Dada ABC

Hours offered: 6-9pm Beijing time during weekdays, plus morning beijing hours on weekends.
Requires TEFL Cert?: Yes.
Requires Native English Speakers?: Yes
Acceptable accents:
Requires College Degree?: Yes.
Requires you to live in a specific country?: No.
Experience with kids/teaching required: Some experience required.
Internet Speed required: They say 10 down, 2 up,
Computer Specs required:
Children or adults :Children
Company books lessons or Parents/Students book lessons: The company does.
Regular students?: Yes.
Average time to be fully booked: Immediately - 1 month.
Flexibility/cancellation policies: Flexible.
Group classes or individual: Individual.
Curriculum type and quality: Mediocre content but teacher-organized activities encouraged.

Browser-based, other platform-based, or company app: Company app on the PC.

Pay Rate: $15 - $26/hour.

Pay Methods offered and Fees: They offer paypal or bank transfer.

Pay Frequency: They pay monthly around the middle of the month for the month before.

Trial class conversion Bonuses: Around $7 depending on the exchange rate, I believe.

Offered Contract Lengths: 6 months - a year.

Gogokid

Minimum Hours: None.

Hours offered: Midnight–8 AM and 8PM–midnight EST

Requires TEFL Cert?: Yes.

Requires Native English Speakers?: Yes

Acceptable accents: Neutral American

Requires College Degree?: Yes

Requires you to live in a specific country?: No but must be legally able to work in US/Canada

Experience with kids/teaching required: Preferred

Internet Speed required: 20 Mbps DL

Computer Specs required: Mac OS 10.8x or higher or Windows 7, Windows 8, Windows 10 or higher, at least 4GB RAM, Intel Core i3.

Children or adults: Children

Company books lessons or Parents/Students book lessons: Parents

Regular students?: Depends on the student/parents.

Average time to be fully booked: 2 weeks

Flexibility/cancellation policies: If you cancel with at least 24 hours notice, you lose one point of your "credit score." Within 24 hours or no-show loses you more points.

Group classes or individual: Individual
Curriculum type and quality: Interactive slides with characters, songs, and animations, some scribbling on the slides
Class Length: 25 mins
Feedback Required?: Yes.
Browser-based, other platform-based, or company app: Browser
Pay Rate: : $8 USD base pay, $10 bonus if trial class converts, once "credit score" reaches 110, $8.80 USD base pay, once credit score reaches 120, $10 USD
Pay Methods offered and Fees: Paypal
Pay Frequency: 15th of the month (for previous month)
Referral Bonuses: $100
Trial class conversion Bonuses: $10
Offered Contract Lengths: 6 months

Printed by Amazon Italia Logistica S.r.l.
Torrazza Piemonte (TO), Italy

13637744R00055